NEW REVISED EDITION

Volume Two

All American Folk
Complete Sheet Music Editions

D1158752

Catalog #07-1060

ISBN# 1-56922-041-7

Printed in the United States of America

Produced by John L. Haag

Exclusive Distributor:
CREATIVE CONCEPTS PUBLISHING CORP.
2290 Eastman Ave., #110, Ventura, California 93003

CONTENTS

CONTENTS

American Folk Trilogy

Slowly

Oh, I wish I was in the land of cot-ton,——
Dix - ie-land, that's where I was born,——

Old times there are not for - got - ten,—— { Look a - way, look a -
Ear - ly, Lord, one fros ty morn-in'—— {

- way, look a - way! Dix - ie - land.——

The Battle Of New Orleans

Words and Music by Jimmy Driftwood

Abilene

2. Sit alone every night,
   Watch the trains roll out of sight,
   Don't I wish they were carrying me
   To Abilene, My Abilene.

3. Crowded city - ain't nothin' free;
   Ain't nothin' in this crowd for me,
   Wish to my God that I could be
   In Abilene, my Abilene.

The Bay Of Mexico

Moderately

2. When I was a young man in my prime,
   Hey-o Suziannah,
   I took them young gals two at a time,
   Round the Bay of Mexico.

   Chorus

3. The reason those pretty gals love me so,
   Hey-o Suziannah,
   'Cause I don't talk everything that I know,
   Round the Bay of Mexico.

   Chorus

Blow Away The Morning Dew

1. There was a farm-er's son who led a hum-ble life, One day in May, he strolled a-way to find him-self a wife, Sing-ing:

Blow a-way the morn-ing dew, the grey morn-ing dew,

Blow a - way the morn - ing dew and let the sun come through. 2. While through.

2. While walking toward the town, he somehow took a look,
And saw a fair young maiden bathing in a woodland brook, He sang:
Blow away the morning dew, the gray morning dew,
Blow away the morning dew and let the sun come through.

3. She quickly donned a dress, this girl of grace and charm,
The lad approached and smiled at her and took her by the arm, Singing:
Blow away the morning dew, the gray morning dew,
Blow away the morning dew and let the sun come through.

4. Less than an hour went by, and love they both could see,
Oh be my bride, he gently sighed, though all I have is me, Singing:
Blow away the morning dew, the gray morning dew,
Blow away the morning dew and let the sun come through.

5. I care not what you own, the maiden then replied,
My father is a wealthy Lord and I will be thy bride, Singing:
Blow away the morning dew, the gray morning dew,
Blow away the morning dew and let the sun come through.

6. They mounted on a milk white steed and to the castle rode,
Though willingly she would have gone to share his poor abode, Singing:
Blow away the morning dew, the gray morning dew,
Blow away the morning dew and let the sun come through.

Boll Weevil

1. The boll wee-vil is a lit-tle black bug, Came from Mex-i-co, they
2. The first time I seen a boll wee-vil He's a-sit-tin' on the

say, All the way to Tex-as Just a-
square; Next time I seen the wee-vil He had

look-in' for a place to stay. Just a-look-in' for a home,
all his fam-'ly there. Just a-look-in' for a home,

3. The farmer said to the weevil,
   "What makes your head so red?"
   The boll weevil said to the farmer,
   "It's a wonder I ain't dead.
      Just a-lookin' for a home. . ."

4. The farmer took the weevil
   And shoved him in hot sand;
   The weevil said to the farmer,
   "I'll stand it like a man.
      It'll be my home. . ."

5. The farmer took the weevil
   And set him on the ice;
   The boll weevil said to the farmer,
   "This is cool and mighty nice.
      It'll be my home. . ."

6. The farmer took the weevil
   And fed him on Paris Green;
   The weevil said to the farmer,
   "That's the best I've ever seen.
      It'll be my home. . ."

7. The boll weevil said to the farmer,
   "You'd better leave me alone;
   I et up all your cotton
   And now I'll eat your corn.
      I'll have a home. . ."

8. The farmer said to the merchant,
   "We're in an awful fix;
   The boll weevil et all the cotton up
   And lef' us only sticks.
      We got no home. . ."

9. The merchant got half the cotton,
   The weevil got the rest;
   Didn't leave the farmer's wife
   But one old calico dress.
      And it's full of holes. . .

10. And if anybody should ax you
    Who was it writ this song,
    It was the farmer man,
    With all but his ov'ralls gone,
       Just a-lookin' for a home. . .

Brown Eyed Girl

Words and Music by Van Morrison

2. Whatever happened to Tuesday and so slow
    Going down the old mine with a transistor radio
    Standing in the sunlight laughing
    Hiding behind a rainbow's wall
    Slipping and a-sliding
    All along the water fall
    With you, my Brown Eyed Girl
    You, my Brown Eyed Girl.
    Do you remember when we used to sing:
    Sha la la (etc.)

3. So hard to find my way, now that I'm all on my own
    I saw you just the other day, my, how you have grown
    Cast my memory back there, Lord
    Sometime I'm overcome thinking 'bout
    Making love in the green grass
    Behind the stadium
    With you, my Brown Eyed Girl
    With you, my Brown Eyed Girl.
    Do you remember when we used to sing:
    Sha la la (etc.)

The Colorado Trail

Smoothly

mf

Weep all ye lit - tle rains, Wail, wind, wail, All a - long, a-long, a-long the Col - o - rad - o trail.

Eyes like a morn-ing star, Lips like a rose, Jen-nie was a pret-ty gal. God Al-might-y knows!

Weep all ye lit - tle rains, Wail, wind, wail, All a-long, a-long, a-long the Col - o - rad - o trail.

Burning Bridges

Words and Music by Walter Scott

Moderately

Verse:

Found some let-ters____ you wrote me, this morn-ing, _____ They
Sold the house____ we once planned to-geth-er, _____ Said good-

told of the love we once knew; _____ Now they're gone____ I
bye to the folks we once knew; _____ Then I moved to a

burned them to ash-es, _____ Don't want none to re-mind me of
far a-way cit-y, _____ Try-ing hard to for-get a-bout

Casey Jones

Moderately, with a strongly marked rhythm

Some folks say Ca - sey Jones can't run,

Stop and lis - ten what Ca - sey done, He left Mem-phis at a

quar - ter to nine, Made New - port News____ 'fore

din - ner time, 'Fore din - ner time, 'fore din - ner time, ___ Made ___

New - port News ___ 'fore din - ner time

2. Casey Jones, before he died,
Fixed the blinds so the bums couldn' ride,
'If they ride, gotta ride the rod,
Trust their life in the hands of God.
In the hands of God, the hands of God,
Trust their life in the hands of God.'

3. There was a woman named Alice Fly,
Said, 'I'm gonna ride with Mr. Casey or die,
I ain't good lookin' but I takes my time,
I'm a ramblin' woman with a ramblin' mind,
With a ramblin' mind,' etc.

4. Early one mornin', 'bout four o'clock,
Told his fireman, 'Get the boiler hot,
All I need's a little water and coal,
Peep out my window, see the drivers roll,
See the drivers roll, etc.

5. He looked at his watch and his watch was slow,
He looked at the water and the water was low.
But the people all knew by the engine's moan,
That the man at the throttle was Casey Jones,
Was Casey Jones, etc.

6. When he come within a mile of the place,
Old Number Four stared him right in the face.
Told his fireman, 'Just keep your seat and ride,
It's a double track road, running side by side,
Runnin' side by side,' etc.

7. You ought to been there to see the sight,
Screamin' an' cryin', both coloured and white,
And I was a witness for the fact,
They flagged Mister Casey, but he never looked back,
But he never looked back, etc.

8. 'Mama, mama have you heard the news,
Papa got killed on the C. B. and Qs' *
'Quit cryin', children, and don't do that,
You've got another papa on the same durn track,
On the same durn track,' etc.

*The Cincinnati, Burlington, and Quincy Railfoad

The Cat Came Back

Mysteriously

Old Mis-ter John-son had trou-bles of his own, He had a yel-low cat which

would-n't leave its home; He tried and he tried to give the cat a-way, He

gave it to a man go-ing far, far a-way. But the cat came back the

ver - y next day, The cat came back, they thought he was a gon-er but the

cat came back, It just could-n't stay a - way.

The man around the corner swore he'd kill the cat on sight,
He loaded up his shotgun with nails and dynamite;
He waited and he waited for the cat to come around,
Ninety-seven pieces of the man is all they found.

He gave it to a little boy with a dollar note,
Told him for to take it up the river in a boat;
They tied a rope around its neck, it must have weighed a pound,
Now they drag the river for a little boy that's drowned.

He gave it to a man going up in a balloon,
He told him for to take it to the man in the moon,
The balloon came down about ninety miles away,
Where he is now, well I dare not say.

He gave it to a man going way out west,
Told him for to take it to the one he loved the best;
First the train hit the curve, then it jumped the rail,
Not a soul was left behind to tell the gruesome tale.

The cat it had some company one night out in the yard,
Someone threw a boot-jack, and they threw it mighty hard,
It caught the cat behind the ear, she thought it rather slight,
When along came a brick-bat and knocked the cat out of sight.

Away across the ocean they did send the cat at last,
Vessel only out a day and making the water fast;
People all began to pray, the boat began to toss,
A great big gust of wind came by and every soul was lost.

On a telegraph wire, sparrows sitting in a bunch,
The cat was feeling hungry, thought she'd like 'em for a lunch;
Climbing softly up the pole, and when she reached the top,
Put her foot upon the electric wire, which tied her in a knot.

Coplas

lai   la   la   la   lai   la   la   la   la.

Literal translation:

You asked for green pepper,
I'll give you green pepper.
Let's go to the garden
And I'll pick it for you.

Dicen que los de tu casa
Ninguno me puede ver,
Diles que no batan l'agua,
Que al cabo lo han de beber.

La mujer que quiere a dos
Los quiere como hermanitos.
Al uno le pone cuernos
Y al otro lo pitoncitos.

La mula que yo monte
La monta hoy mi compadre,
Eso a mi no me importa
Pues yo la monte primero.

La noche que me casa,
No pude dormirme un rato
Por estrar toda la noche
Corriendo detra de un gato.

Me dijiste gue fue un gato
El que entro por tu balcon
Yo no he visto gato prieto
Con sombrero y pantalon.

They say your family
Can't stand to see me.
Tell them not to muddy the water;
In the end they'll have to drink it.

The woman who loves two men
Loves them like brothers.
She puts big horns on one
And budding horns on the other.

The mule I used to ride
Is now ridden by my friend;
I don't care
Because I broke her in.

The night I got married
I couldn't sleep all night.
I spent the whole night
Chasing a black cat.

You said it was a black cat
That came in through your balcony.
I've never seen a black cat before
Wearing a hat and trousers.

Until It's Time For You To Go

Words and Music by Buffy Sainte-Marie

Here Comes The Sun

Words and Music by George Harrison

Sun, sun, sun, Here it comes.

comes.

Here Comes The Sun, Here Comes The Sun, It's all-right.

It's all-right.

Dry Bones

Allegro con moto

E - ze-kiel con-nect-ed them Dry__ Bones, E - ze-kiel con-nect-ed them

Dry__ Bones, E - ze - kiel con-nect - ed them Dry__ Bones, I

(Augment tempo and sound gradually)

hear the word of the Lord. Your toe bone con -nect-ed to your

Everybody's Talkin'

Words and Music by Fred Neil

Freight Train

With A Lively Beat

Freight train, freight train run so fast _____

Freight train, freight train run so fast _____

When I am dead and in my grave,
No more good times here I'll crave,
Place the stones at my head and feet
And tell them all that I'm gone to sleep.

When I die, Lord, bury me deep,
Way down on old Chestnut Street,
So I can hear old Number Nine
As she comes rolling by.

When I die, Lord, bury me deep,
Way down on old Chestnut Street,
Place the stones at my head and feet
And tell them all that I'm gone to sleep.

Gee, But I Want To Go Home

Moderately

The cof-fee that they give you, they say is might - y fine, It's good for cuts and bruis-es, And it tastes like i - o - dine.

Chorus: I don't want no more of ar - my life, Gee, but I want to go home.

The biscuits that they give you they say are might fine;
One rolled off a table and it killed a pal of mine,

The chickens that they give you they say are might fine;
One rolled off a table and it started making time.

The details that they give us they say are might fine;
The garbage that we pick up they feed us all the time.

The clothes that they give you they say are mighty fine,
But me and my buddy can both fit into mine.

The women in the service club they say are mighty fine,
But most are over ninety and the rest are under nine.

They treat us all like monkeys and make us stand in line;
They give you fifty dollars and take back forty-nine.

Go Away From My Window

50

Good News

Brightly

1. Goin' to   get up in the char - i - ot, ___ car - ry me home,   Get up in the char - i - ot, ___
2. There's a   long white robe in the heav-en I know,   Long white robe in the
3. There's a   gold - en harp in the heav-en I know,   Gold - en harp in the

car - ry me   home,   Get up   in   the char - i - ot, _____
heav - en I   know,   Long white   robe in the
heav - en I   know,   Gold - en harp in the

D.C. al Fine

car - ry me home,
heav-en I   know, An' I   don't want her leave-a me be - hind.
heav-en I   know,

Green, Green

Words and Music by
Randy Sparks and Barry McGuire

VERSE

1. Well, I told my ma-ma on the day I was born, "Don-cha
2. No, there ain't no-bod-y in this whole _ wide world Gon-na
Optional } → 3. Loved that man _ with _ all _ my heart, _ I _
Girls verse } _ 4. I don't care _ when the sun _ goes down, _ Where I

cry _ when you see I'm gone. _ You know there ain't no wo-man gon-na
tell me how to spend my time. _ _ I'm _ just a good _ lov-in'
will _ till the day I die. _ _ I was just a stop _ a -
lay _ my _ wea-ry head; _ _ Green, green val-ley or a

set-tle me down, _ I just got-ta be trav-el-in' on." _ A - sing-in'
ram-ble-in' man. _ Say Bud-dy, could you spare me a dime? _
long _ his way; _ Nev-er e-ven said _ good-bye. _
rock-y road; _ It's there I'm gon-na make _ my bed. _

Hail, Hail, The Gang's All Here

Hail! Hail! The gang's all here, What the heck do we care, What the heck do we care. Hail! Hail! The gang's all here, What the heck do we care now!

Hey Joe

Words and Music by
Billy Roberts

Bright Rock Beat

HEY JOE___ where ya goin' with that gun in your hand _____ (I said,)

HEY JOE ___ where ya goin' with that gun in your hand _____ I'm go - in'

out and find my wo - man now__ She's been run - nin' 'round with some oth - er man. I said I'm

go - in' out ___ and find my wo - man, she's been run - nin' 'round with some oth - er man.

House Of The Rising Sun

I Am A Pilgrim

Medium tempo

I got a mother, a sister and a brother,
Who have gone to that sweet land,
I'm determined to go and see them,
    good Lord,
All over on that distant shore.

As I go down to that river Jordan,
Just to bathe my weary soul,
If I could touch but the hem of His
    garment, good Lord,
Well, I believe it would make me whole.

I Can See Clearly Now

Words and Music by Jonny Nash

poco dim.

D.S. al Coda

CODA

It's gon-na be a bright, bright —— sun shin- y day.-

Hey Lolly, Lolly

With a Calypso beat

Hey lol - ly, lol - ly, lol - ly, Hey lol - ly, lol - ly, lo____

Hey lol - ly, lol - ly, lol - ly, Hey lol - ly, lol - ly, lo.____

Married men will keep your secret,
Hey lolly, lolly lo.
Single boys will talk about you,
Hey lolly, lolly lo.

Two old maids a-sittin' in the sand. . .
Each one wishin' that the other was a man. . .

I have a girl, she's ten feet tall. . .
Sleeps in the kitchen with her feet in the hall. . .

Everybody sing the chorus. . .
Either you're against us or you're for us. . .

The purpose of this little song. . .
Is to make up verses as you go along. . .

I'd Like To Be In Texas

In a corner in an old arm chair sat a man whose hair was gray,
He had listened to them longingly, to what they had to say.
They asked him where he'd like to be and his clear old voice did ring:
"I'd like to be in Texas for the round-up in the spring.

They all sat still and listened to each word he had to say;
They knew the old man sitting there had once been young and gay.
They asked him for a story of his life out on the plains,
He slowly then removed his hat and quietly began:

"Oh, I've seen them stampede o'er the hills, when you'd think they'd never stop,
I've seen them run for miles and miles until their leader dropped,
I was foreman on a cowranch - that's the calling of a king;
I'd like to be in Texas for the round-up in the spring."

I'd Really Love To See You Tonight

Words and Music by Parker McGee

My Sweet Lord

Words and Music by George Harrison

I'd Like To Teach The World To Sing
(In Perfect Harmony)

Words and Music by B. Backer, B. Davis, R. Cook and R. Greenaway

Jamaica Farewell

Smoothly

In Ja - mai - ca, Ca - lyp - so isle,___ Ev - 'ry -

bod - y danc - ing with a hap - py smile.___ All but a young man a -

long the pier, ___ He had a song to sing ___ that was

Chorus:

sad to hear: ___ I must sail a - way, ___ a -

cross the sea, ___ Leave the girl, ___ who on - ly loves me, ___ Al -

though I say ___ "Fare - well Ja - mai - ca" to - day, ___ I know that

I'll come back to her an - oth - er day. ___

La Bamba

La Cucaracha

Lively

1. Cuan - do u - no quier - e_a u - na   Y es - ta u - na no lo
1. When a fel - low loves a maid - en   And that maid - en does - n't

quier - e,   Es lo mis - mo que si_un cal - vo
love him,   It's the same as when a bald man

Chorus:

En la cal - le_en - cuen - tra_un pei - ne. La cu - ca - rach - a, la cu - ca
Finds a comb up - on the high - way. The cu - ca - rach - a, the cu - ca

A7

rach - a, Ya no quier - e cam - i - nar, Por - que no
rach - a, Does -n't want to trav - el on, Be - cause she

D

tien - e, Por-que le fal - ta, Ma - ri -hua - na que fu - mar.
has - n't, Oh, no she has - n't, Ma - ri -hua - na for to smoke.

2. All the girls up at Las Vegas
   Are most awful tall and skinny,
   But they're worse for plaintive pleading
   Than the souls in Purgatory.
   Chorus

3. All the girls here in the city
   Don't know how to give you kisses,
   While the ones from Albuquerque
   Stretch their necks to avoid misses.
   Chorus

4. One thing makes me laugh most hearty —
   Pancho Villa with no shirt on.
   Now the Carranzistas beat it
   Because Villa's men are coming.
   Chorus

5. Fellow needs an automobile
   If he undertakes the journey
   To the place to which Zapata
   Ordered the famous convention.
   Chorus

Oh, Them Golden Slippers

Brightly

Oh, my gold - en slip-pers are ___ laid a - way, 'Cause I don't 'spect to wear them till my wed - ding day, And my long - tailed coat, that I loved so well, I will wear up in the char - iot in the

Oh, my old banjo hangs on the wall,
'Cause it ain't been tuned since 'way last fall,
But the folks all say we'll have a good time,
When we ride up in the chariot in the morn,
There's old Brother Ben and his sister Luce,
They will telegraph the news to Uncle 'Bacco
What a great camp meeting there will be that day,
When we ride up in the chariot in the morning.

So, it's goodbye children, I will have to go,
Where the rain don't fall and wind don't blow,
And your ulster coats, why, you will not need,
When you ride up in the chariot in the morn,
But your golden slippers must be nice and clean,
And your age must be just sweet sixteen,
And your white kid gloves you will have to wear,
When you ride up in the chariot in the morn.

L'il Liza Jane

Allegretto

1. I know a gal that I a - dore, L'il Li - za Jane.
2. Down where she lives, the po-sies grow, L'il Li - za Jane.
3. I would - n't care how far we roam, L'il Li - za Jane.

'Way down south in Bal - ti - more, L'il Li - za Jane.
Chick - ens 'round the kitch - en door, L'il Li - za Jane.
Where she's at is home sweet home, L'il Li - za Jane.

Chorus

Oh, E - li - za, Li'l Li - za Jane! Oh, E - li - za, L'il Li - za Jane.

Lily Of The West

first I came to Lou-is-ville, Some pleas-ure there to find, A dam-sel there from Lex-ing-ton was pleas-ing to my mind. Her ros-y cheeks, her ru-by lips like ar-rows pierced my

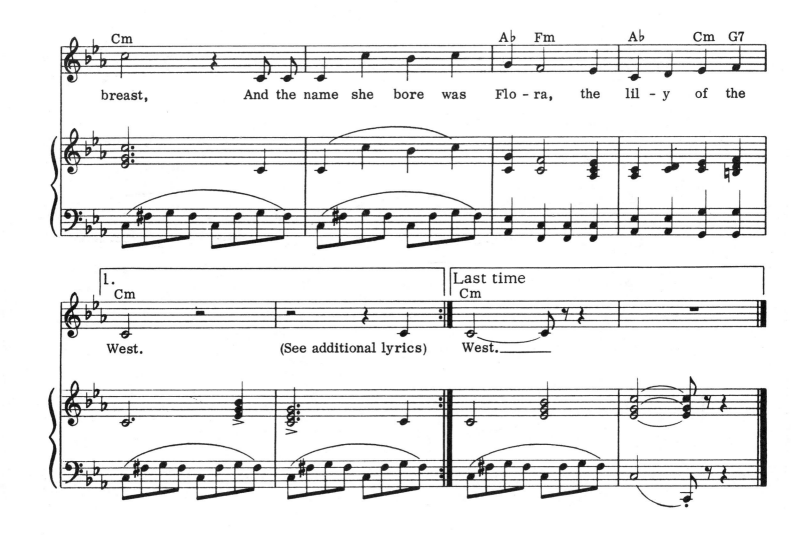

breast, And the name she bore was Flo - ra, the lil - y of the

West. (See additional lyrics) West.____

2. I courted lovely Flora, and to her I was so kind,
   But she went to another man,
   It nearly wrecked my mind.
   She robbed me of my freedom and deprived
        me of my rest,
   Betrayed was I by Flora, the lily of the West.

3. He met her in a shady grove, this man of high
        degree,
   I saw him kiss my Flora and it sure did things
        to me.
   She told me he was just a friend, but still I was
        depressed,
   Betrayed was I by Flora, the lily of the West.

4. I stepped up to my rival with my dagger
        in my hand,
   I seized him by the collar, it's not hard
        to understand,
   That, blinded by my jealousy, I pierce
        him in the breast,
   Betrayed was I by Flora, the lily of the West.

5. The trial was held, I made a plea, but
        'twas of no avail,
   Now I await the hangman in a stinkin'
        rotten jail.
   But, though I give my all away and though
        my life is messed,
   I love my faithless Flora, the lily of the West.

Sunshine (Go Away Today)

Words and Music by Jonathan Edwards

to Coda

these ain't dues___ I been___ pay - in'.
he's got cards___ he ain't___ show - in'.
Brand new bells___ will be___ ring - in'.

to Coda

Chorus

How much does it___ cost?___ I'll buy___ it. The time is all___ we've___ lost.___ I'll try___ it, 'n'

he can't e - ven run___ his own___ life I'll be damned if he'll___ run mine!___

1. 2. *D.S. al Coda*

Sun - shine,___ Sun - shine,___

Coda

D.S. al Coda

Mary Ann

CHORUS

All day, all night, Ma - ry Ann, _____ Down by the sea - side sift- in' sand, _____ All the lit - tle chil - dren love Ma - ry Ann, _____ Down by the sea - side sift -in' sand. _____

2. When I met sweet Mary Ann,
   Her mother said to me:
   Would you care to tell me
   Where you stand financially?
   She does not approve of me,
   'Cause I'm no millionaire,
   But I love her daughter,
   More than I can bear.

   (To CHORUS)

Michael

Brightly

Chorus

MI - CHAEL, row the boat a - shore, Hal - le - lu - jah, MI - CHAEL,

row the boat a - shore, Hal - le - lu - jah.

Sis - ter
The Jor - dan
The Jor - dan

help to trim the sail, Hal - le - lu - jah, Sis - ter,
Riv - er is chil - ly and cold, Hal - le - lu - jah, Kills the
Riv - er is deep and wide, Hal - le - lu - jah, Milk and

Midnight Special

2. Well if you're ever in Houston,
   You'd better walk on by
   Oh, you'd better not gamble, boy
   I say you'd better not fight.
   Well now, the sheriff, he'll grab you
   And his boys will pull you down
   And then before you know it
   You're penitentiary-bound.
       (To Chorus) A-let the Midnight Special etc.

3. Here comes Miss Lucy
   How in the world do you know?
   I know by her apron
   And by the dress she wore.
   An umbrella on her shoulder
   A piece of paper in her hand
   She gonna see the sheriff
   To try to free her man.
       (To Chorus) A-let the Midnight Special etc.

Oh, Mary, Don't You Weep

With tenderness

Oh, Mar-y, don't you weep, don't you mourn, Oh, Mar-y, don't you weep, don't you mourn, Phar-aoh's ar-my got drown - ded, Oh, Mar-y, don't you

weep.

If I could I sure - ly would___

Stand on the rock where Mo - ses stood.

Phar-aoh's ar - my got

drown - ded.

Oh,

Mar - y, don't you weep.

Moses stood on the Red Sea shore,
Smitin' that water with a two-by-four.

Pharaoh's army got drownded,
Oh, Mary, don't you weep.

God gave Noah the rainbow sign,
"No more water, but fire next time!"...

One of these nights, about twelve o'clock
This old world's gonna reel and rock...

I may be right and I may be wrong,
I know you're gonna miss me when I'm gone...

Third-Rate Romance

Words and Music by Russell Smith

low-rent ren - dez-vous.____
low-rent ren - dez-vous.____

Third - rate ro - mance, low - rent ren - dez - vous;__

____ third-rate ro - mance,

low - rent ren - dez - vous.____

Rock About My Saro Jane

O there's noth - ing to do but to
set down and sing And rock a - bout _____ my
Sa - ro Jane. _____

2. Boiler busted and the whistle done blowed,
   The head captain done fell overboard.
   O Saro Jane!

3. Engine gave a crack and the whistle gave a squall,
   The engineer gone to the hole in the wall.
   O Saro Jane.

4. Yankees built boats for to shoot them rebels,
   My musket's loaded and I'm gonna hold her level.
   O Saro Jane!

Old Mountain Dew

Adapted by Woody Hayes

On And On

Words and Music by Stephen Bishop

The Other Side Of This Life

Words and Music by Fred Neil

Plastic Jesus

With a steady beat

I don't care if it rains or freez - es
Through my trials and trib - u - la - tions

Long as I've got my plas - tic Je - sus
And my trav - els through the na - tions

Rid - ing on the dash - board of my

car;

With my plas - tic Je - sus I'll go

far. Plas-tic Je - sus, plas-tic Je - sus,

Rid-ing on the dash-board of my car; I'm a - fraid He'll have to go, His

mag-nets ruin my ra - di - o, And if I have a wreck, He'll leave a scar.

Riding down a thoroughfare, With His nose up in the air,
A wreck may be ahead, but He don't mind,
Trouble coming He don't see, He just keeps His eye on me,
And any other thing that lies behind.

When pedestrians try to cross, I let them know who's boss,
I never blow the horn or give them warning;
I ride all over town, trying to run them down,
And it's seldom that they live to see the morning.

Plastic Jesus, Plastic Jesus,
Riding on the dashboard of my car;
Though the sunshine on His back,
Makes Him peel, chip and crack
A little patching keeps Him up to par.

Plastic Jesus, Plastic Jesus,
Riding on the dashboard of my car;
His halo fits just right
And I use it for a sight,
And they'll scatter or they'll splatter near and far.

Roll In My Sweet Baby's Arms

Adapted by Slim Martin

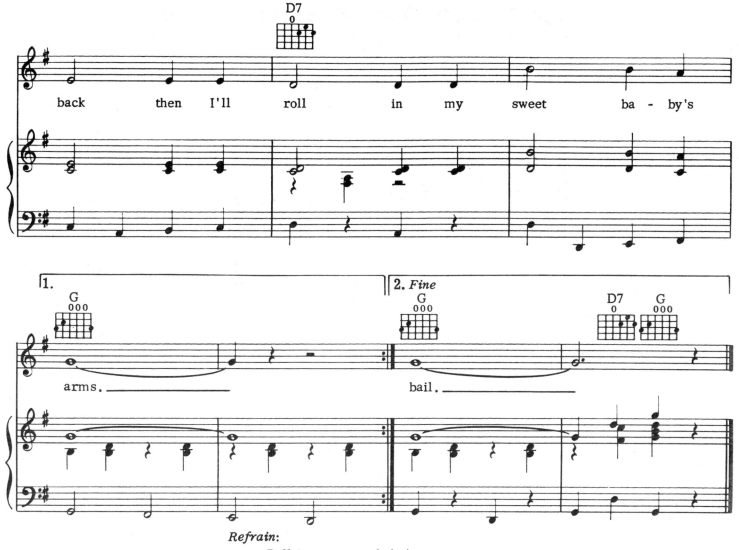

back then I'll roll in my sweet ba - by's

1.
arms.

2. *Fine*
bail.

Refrain:

Roll in my sweet baby's arms,
Roll in my sweet baby's arms,
Lay 'round the shack 'til the mail train comes back,
Then I'll roll in my sweet baby's arms.

Can't see what's the matter with my own true love,
She done quit writing to me,
She must think I don't love her like I used to,
Ain't that a foolish idea.

Sometimes there's a change in the ocean,
Sometimes there's a change in the sea,
Sometimes there's a change in my own true love,
But there's never no change in me.

Mama's a ginger-cake baker,
Sister can weave and can spin,
Dad's got an interest in that old cotton mill,
Just watch that old money roll in.

They tell me that your parents do not like me,
They have drove me away from your door,
If I had all my time to do over,
I would never go there any more.

Now where was you last Friday night,
While I was locked up in jail,
Walking the streets with another man,
Wouldn't even go my bail.

Rye Whisky

Adapted by Slim Martin

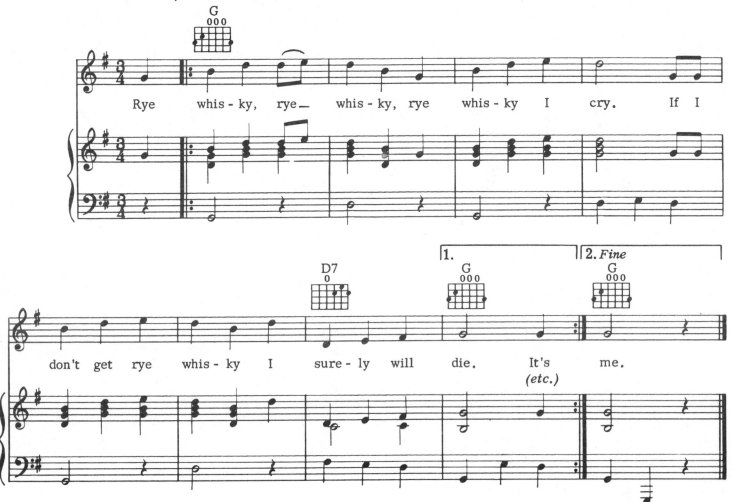

It's whisky, rye whisky,
I know you of old,
You robbed my poor pockets
Of silver and gold.

It's beefsteak when I'm hungry,
Rye whisky when I'm dry,
A greenback when I'm hard up,
Oh, Heaven when I die.

I go to yonder holler
And I'll build me a still,
And I'll give you a gallon
For a five-dollar bill.

If the ocean was whisky
And I was a duck,
I'd dive to the bottom
And never come up.

But the ocean ain't whisky,
And I ain't a duck.
So I'll play Jack o' Diamonds
And trust to my luck.

Her parents don't like me,
They say I'm too poor,
And that I am unfit
To darken her door.

Her parents don't like me,
Well, my money's my own,
And them that don't like me
Can leave me alone.

Oh whisky, you villain,
You're no friend to me,
You killed my poor pappy,
God-damn you, try me.

Santy Anno

Moderately

We're sail-ing down the riv-er from Liv-er - pool, Heave a - way, San - ty An - no! _____ A-

round Cape Horn to Fric - co Bay, All___ on the plains of Mex - i - co.

So heave her up and away we go,
Heave away, Santy Anno!
Heave her up and away we go,
All on the plains of Mexico.

She's a fast clipper ship and a bully good crew. . .
A down-east Yankee for her captain,

There's plenty of gold, so I've been told. . .
There's plenty of gold, so I've been told. . .

Back in the days of Forty-Nine. . .
Those were the days of the good old times. . .

When Zacharias Taylor gained the day. . .
He made poor Santy run away. . .

General Scott and Taylor, too. . .
Made poor Santy meet his Waterloo. . .

Santy Anno was a good old man. . .
Till he got into war with your Uncle Sam. . .

When I leave this ship I will settle down. . .
And marry a girl named Sally Brown. . .

Saturday Night

Words and Music by Randy Sparks

CHORUS

Sat-ur-day Night,_ Sat-ur-day Night,_ We all_ get to-geth-er on Sat-ur-day Night_

1.3.{ Put on yer shoes, go down_ town,_ do noth-in' but walk a-round.}
2. {Look at the girls, then what do we do?_ Turn a-round, see if they're look-in' too.} On a

Sun-day or a Mon-day you can't_ do it right. Ain-cha glad we got Sat-ur-day Night?_

VERSE

1. Ear-ly in the eve-nin', _____ all week_ long,_ Sit on the stoop and sing your lit-tle song.
2. Old _____ tim-ers down at Led - bet-ter store_ Tell ya young folks ain't like they were be-fore. They're
3. Sat-ur-day eve - nin', when the work's all _ done_ Come on a - long, we'll have a lit-tle fun.

Scarborough Fair

Slowly, with feeling

Are you go - ing to Scar - bor - ough
Tell her to make me a cam - bric

Fair? Pars - ley, sage, _____ rose -
shirt, Pars - ley, sage, _____ rose -

ma - ry and thyme; Re - mem - ber
ma - ry and thyme; With - out any

Pars - ley, sage,_____ rose - ma - ry and thyme; be -
Pars - ley, sage,_____ rose - ma - ry and thyme; and

tween the sea foam _____ and the sea sand ____ Or
tie it all up with a pea - cock's feath - er, Or

nev - er be a true love of mine.
nev - er be a true love of mine.

rit.

See See Rider

Sloop John B

1. We come on the SLOOP JOHN B. my grand - fa - ther and
(2. The) first mate, he got drunk. Broke in the Cap - tain's
(3. The) poor cook, he got took fits. Throw a - way all the

me A - round Nas - sau Town we did roam.
trunk. Con - sta - ble had to come and take him a - way.
grits. Then he took and ate up all of the corn.

Drink - ing all night, we got in a fight,
Sher - iff John Stone, please let me a - lone,
Sher - iff John Stone, please let me a - lone,

Sinner Man

Moderately

Oh, sin - ner man,

where you gon - na run to;

Oh, sin - ner man, where you gon - na

Run to the rock, the rock was a-melting,   (3)

Run to the sea, the sea was a-boiling,   (3)

Run to the moon, the moon was a-bleeding,   (3)

Run to the Lord, Lord won't you hide me?   (3)

Run to the Devil, Devil was a-waiting,   (3)

Oh sinner man, you oughta been a-praying.   (3)

St. James Infirmary

The Strawberry Roan

Moderately

C

I was hang-in' 'round town just a - spend-ing my time.
"You guessed me right, and a good one," I claim,

G7

Noth-ing else
Do you hap-pen to

C

to spend not ev - en a dime, When a fel - ler steps up and he
have an - y bad ones to tame?" He ___ says, "I've got one, and a

F

says, "I sup - pose you're a bronc-bust-in' man ___ by the looks of your clothes."
bad one to buck; At ___ throw-in' bronc rid - ers, he's ___ had lots of

G7

1.

luck, Well, it's Oh, that straw - ber - ry roan! _____

Oh, that straw - ber - ry roan! _____ He says, "This old

po - ny ain't nev - er been rode, And the boy that gets on him is

sure to get throwed," Oh, that straw - ber - ry roan! _____

I gets all excited and asks what he pays
To ride this old goat for a couple of days.
He offers a ten spot. I says, "I'm your man,
"For the bronc never lived that I couldn't fan;
"No, the bronc never lived, nor he never drew breath
"That I couldn't ride till he starved plumb to death."
He say, "Get your saddle, I'll give you a chance."
We got in the buckboard and drove to the ranch.

. . .We stayed until morning, and right after chuck
We goes out to see how this outlaw can buck,
Oh, that strawberry roan.

Well, down in the horse corral standing alone
Was that old cavayo, old strawberry roan,
His legs were spavined and he had pigeon toes,
Little pig eyes and a big Roman nose.
Little pin ears that were crimped at the tip,
With a big "forty-four" branded 'cross his left hip.
He's ewe-necked and old, with a long lower jaw,
You can see with one eye he's a reg'lar outlaw.

. . .He's ewe-necked and old, with a long lower jaw,
You can see with one eye he's a reg'lar outlaw,
Oh, that strawberry roan.

Well, I put on my spurs and I coils up my twine,
I piled my loop on him — I'm sure feeling fine.
I piled my loop on him and well I knew then,
If I rode this old pony, I'd sure earn my ten.
I put the blinds on him — it sure was a fight,
Next comes the saddle, I screws her down tight.
I gets in his middle and opens the blind,
I'm right in his middle to see him unwind.

. . .He lowered his neck and I think he unwound,
He seemed to quit living there down on the ground,
Oh, that strawberry roan.

He went up towards the east and came down towards the west,
To stay in his middle I'm doin' my best.
He's about the worst bucker I've seen on the range —
He can turn on a nickel and give you some change,
He turns his old belly right up to the sun,
He sure is one sun-fishin' son of a gun!
I'll tell you, no foolin', this pony can step,
But I'm still in his middle and buildin' a rep.

. . .He goes up on all fours and comes down on his side,
I don't see what keeps him from losing his hide.
Oh, that strawberry roan!

I loses my stirrup and also my hat,
I starts pulling leather, I'm blind as a bat.
With a big forward jump he goes up on high,
Leaves me sittin' on nothin' way up in the sky.
I turns over twice and comes back to the earth,
I lights in a-cussin' the day of his birth.
I know there are ponies I'm unable to ride —
Some are still living, they haven't all died.

. . .I'll bet all my money the man ain't alive
That can stay with old strawberry making his dive,
Oh, that strawberry roan!

(There Was A) Tall Oak Tree

Words and Music by Dorsey Burnette

Sweet Betsy From Pike

Moderate Waltz Tempo

VERSE

Did you ev - er hear tell of sweet Bet - sy from Pike? She

crossed the wide prai - ries with her hus - band, Ike. With two yoke of

ox - en and one spot - ted hog, And a fat Shang - hai roos - ter, an

CHORUS

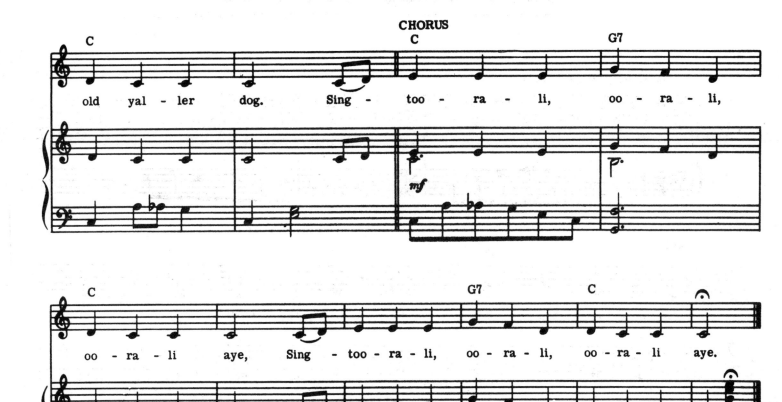

old yal - ler dog. Sing - too - ra - li, oo - ra - li,

oo - ra - li aye, Sing - too - ra - li, oo - ra - li, oo - ra - li aye.

2. One evening quite early they camped by
a stream.
To reach California, oh that was their
dream.
The Shanghai was "et" but the cattle just
died,
The last strip of bacon that morning was
fried.   (Chorus)

3. Came the Injuns from nowhere, a wild
yelling horde,
And Betsy was skeered as she prayed to
the Lord.
Behind their big wagon the couple did
crawl,
And they fought off the Injuns with musket
and ball.   (Chorus)

4. Then they swam the wide rivers and crossed
the tall peaks,
And lived on wild berries and water for
weeks.
Starvation and hard work and sun-stroke as
well,
But they reached California in spite of
all hell.   (Chorus)

5. They were six months in Frisco,
when Ike met a girl,
A sweet looking dancer who gave
him a twirl.
He spoke of poor Betsy as "just an
old horse",
What was Betsy to do? She gave Ike
his divorce.   (Chorus)

6. She left Frisco and went back to
Pike, so they say,
And Ike lost his dancer and soon
passed away.
If this tale is touching, go cry if
you like
Mighty fine kind of woman!
Sweet Betsy from Pike. (Chorus)

Tell Old Bill

leave them down - town gals a - lone, _____ This morn - ing, _____ this eve - ning, _____ so _____ soon. _____

Old Sal was baking bread, this morning,
Old Sal was baking bread, this evening,
Old Sal was baking bread,
When she found out her Bill was dead,
This morning, this evening, so soon.

She said, "Oh, no, it can't be so". . .
"My Bill left here about an hour ago."
She said, "Oh, no, this can't be". . .
They killed my Bill in the third degree."

Well, they brought Bill home in a hurry-up wagon. . .
Poor dead Bill, how his toes were draggin'.

We'll Sing In The Sunshine

Words and Music by Gale Garnett

Whistling Gypsy Rover

Moderately

Verse

1. The gyp-sy ro-ver come o-ver the hill, Bound through the val-ley so sha-dy; He
2. left her fa-ther's ___ cas-tle ___ gate, She left her own true ___ lov-er; She
3. fa-ther sad-dled his fast-est ___ steed, Roamed the ___ val-ley all o-ver; ___
4. came at last to a man-sion ___ fine, Down by the ri-ver ___ Clayde; ___ And
5. He's no gyp-sy my fa-ther, said she, My lord of free-lands all o-ver; And

whist-led and he sang till the green woods rang, And he won the heart of a la - dy. ___
left ___ her ___ ser-vants and her es-tate, To fol-low the gyp-sy ___ ro-ver. ___
Sought ___ his ___ daugh-ter at great ___ speed, And the WHIST-LING GYP-SY ___ RO-VER. ___
there ___ was ___ mu-sic and there was wine, For the gyp-sy and his ___ la - dy. ___
I ___ will ___ stay till my dy-ing day, With my WHIST-LING GYP-SY ___ RO-VER. ___

Will The Circle Be Unbroken?

by Sarah Mills

1. There are loved ones in the glo - ry Whose dear forms you oft - en
2. joy - ous days of child - hood Oft they told of won - drous
3. mem - ber songs of heav - en which you sang with child - ish
4. pic - ture hap - py gath - 'rings 'round the fire - side long a -
5. one their seats were emp - tied, One by one they went a -

miss. When you close your earth - ly sto - ry Will you
love. Point - ed to the dy - ing Sav - iour, Now they
voice. Do you love the hymns they taught you, Or are
go, And you think of tear - ful part - ings When they
way. Now the fam - i - ly is part - ed. Will it

join them in their bliss?_____
dwell with Him a - bove._____
songs of earth your choice?_____
left you here be - low._____
be com -plete one day?_____

Will the cir - cle be un-

brok - en By and by,_____ by and by, In a bet - ter home a-

wait - ing In the sky, in the sky?_____

2. In the sky?
3. You re-
4. You can
5. One by

You're A Flower In The Wildwood

By Del Holiday

Lively

On one eve-ning long a - go, when th

sun was sink-in' low. My true lov-er went to sail up-on the sea. It was

in the month of June when the ros - es were in bloom And he took me in his arms and said to

Chorus:

me: You're a flow - er bloomin' in the wild - wood, a

flow - er bloom-in' there for me, Sweet-er than the morn-ing dew, and I'll

soon re - turn to you you're a flow'r that is bloom-ing there for me.

2. Then this message came to me
   From the captain on the sea
   And it told me that my darlin' was dead

   Oh the shocking words surprised
   Brought the teardrops to my eyes
   When I thought about the last words that I said *(Chorus)*

3. Now he can't return to me
   He got drowned in the sea
   And he's past over life's weary way

   When it's in the month of June
   And the roses are in bloom
   Oh it seems that I can hear my darling say *(Chorus)*

You Better Move On

Words and Music by Arthur Alexander

Moderately

You ask me to give up the hand of the girl I love,
know you can buy her fan-cy clothes___ and ___ dia-mond rings,
think you'd bet-ter go now I'm get-tin'___ might-y mad,

You tell me I'm not the man she's
But I be-lieve she's hap-py with me with-
You ask me to give up the on-ly love I

worth-y of. _____
out those things. _____
ev - er had. _____

But who are you _
Still you beg me _
May be I would _

Last time To Coda

_____ to tell her who to love?_____ That's
_____ oh, to set her free,_____ But my friend that'll
_____ oh, but I love her so,_____ I'm nev-er gon-na

up to her,_____ yes___ and the Lord a-bove,_____

Something

Words and Music by George Harrison

Some-thing in the way__ she moves__

Instrumental

at - tracts me like no oth - er lov - er,

Some-thing in the way she woos__